Room Parent's
PARTY PLANNER

HOW TO HOST GREAT PARTIES
IN YOUR CHILD'S CLASSROOM

by Lynn Basow

1

DEDICATION

To my parents, Fred and Charlotte Doepke
Principal and Teacher

THANKS TO:

Chuck Marsh,
for the words.

Dan Wallace,
for the pictures.

Dan Reeder,
for the advice.

My husband Bob,
for the encouragement.

My daughters,
Annie and Lucy,
for the opportunity.

SPECIAL THANKS TO:

Linda Herbel and her team
at Quail Run School
in Lawrence, Kansas,
and to the many room parents
with whom I've shared

IBSN 0-9638975-0-0 9.95
Published by: Inverness Press
P.O. Box 1174 Lawrence, KS 66044
FAX: 913-843-2640

TABLE OF CONTENTS

INTRODUCTION   A Little Encouragement
                      and Reassurance   **4**

CHAPTER   1   What is a Room Party   **6**

CHAPTER   2   Teamwork   **10**

CHAPTER   3   Specific Room Parties   **19**

CHAPTER   4   Room Party Timelines   **23**

CHAPTER   5   Snacks, Crafts & Games,
                      an Introduction   **31**

CHAPTER   6   Snacks, Crafts & Games,
                      Kindergarten through
                      2nd Grade   **38**

CHAPTER   7   Snacks, Crafts & Games,
                      Third & Fourth Grades   **43**

CHAPTER   8   Snacks, Crafts & Games,
                      Fifth & Sixth Grades   **49**

CHAPTER   9   Common Questions
                      and Answers   **53**

CHAPTER   10   Conclusion   **55**

INTRODUCTION

A Little Encouragement and Reassurance

RELAX!

That's my most important advice to you on room parenting. Relax: You can do it. You're even going to have fun!

* Usually we're talking about only three parties a year: Halloween, Winter (Christmas) and Valentine's Day. Some planning and preparation time is required, of course. But being a room parent is not a daily or even weekly commitment.

* Room parties usually are at the end of the school day, which can be easier to fit into your schedule, whether you work at home or in an office. Let's face it: For especially busy room parents, there's never a completely convenient time for a classroom party. But the end of the school day is probably the least inconvenient.

* I truly believe that room parties should be easy and almost free. They should not involve a lot of work, nor should they involve a lot of money. Recruiting several parent volunteers for each party can minimize effort and expense and maximize fun. Spread the word and spread the work!

Do you know what the worst two things about room parenting may be? The shock of being back in a grade-school and the disappointment of would-be room parents who weren't able to help.

* My husband, Bob, and I recently invited a friend to a classroom party. He and his wife have a young son, and their room-parenting years are just ahead of them. He hadn't set foot in a grade school for probably 25 years, so we warned him about "grade-school flashback," the tidal wave of memories, good and bad, that can engulf you when you return to a grade-school for the first time as an adult. He told us that, even with our warning, he almost got dizzy as he entered the school. The long hallways, the smells, the bulletin boards with announcements and assignments uncovered feelings buried for decades. It wasn't a bad experience, he said, but it was intense. It doesn't happen to everyone, but our friend is a

believer in "grade-school flashback."

☛ The worst thing that has ever happened to me as a room parent is facing the disappointment of parents who wanted to help but didn't get the note from their children. Or perhaps they missed the open house where volunteers were recruited. I wouldn't belittle their disappointment for a moment, but if that's the worst thing that's happened to me in nine years of room parenting, you can see why I know you're going to be a great room parent—and you're going to have fun.

If I were you at this point, I'd be wondering who Lynn Basow is and why she thinks she knows so much about room parties. My best qualifications, I think, aren't my two university degrees in education; they're my two daughters, Annie and Lucy. They're two years apart, and I've been a room parent for each in kindergarten through sixth grade. In other words, I've had nine years of seeing what works and what doesn't. If a room-party game or snack didn't work for Annie's class, I refined it by the time Lucy's classmates encountered it.

I've also spent 20-plus years as a full-time or substitute teacher in grade schools, and I come from a family of teachers. But this book is not meant to lay down the law. Being flexible is the key to creating a good party at which you and the kids will have fun. I hope you'll use my suggestions as guidelines only, not as ancient laws written in stone.

My goal in this introduction, honestly, is to encourage and reassure you about being a room parent. So please forgive my immodesty if I share a personal success story with you, one that can someday be your story, too. "Oh, boy," shouted one of my daughter Lucy's classmates on the first day of third grade. "I'm in your room. Your mom better be one of our room parents!"

Let me tell you, that feels good.

CHAPTER ONE

What Is a Room Party?

So what exactly is a room party?

Let's start with a comparison to something familiar: a birthday party. A room party is like a birthday party in several ways:

- each usually involves a fairly large group of children
- each involves games
- each involves food
- each involves a festive atmosphere

But there are important differences between a room party and a birthday party. With a room party:

- you don't create the guest list
- the spotlight isn't on just one child (your child!). Instead, all the children must participate equally
- there usually are no gifts
- time may be in shorter supply; room parties usually last only an hour or less
- the children's teacher is present

And you know what? A room party isn't nearly as time consuming or emotionally charged as a birthday party.

In a nutshell, a room party:

- involves all the children in a classroom
- usually takes place in the classroom (the school gym can be an exciting alternative)
- usually involves three elements: snacks, crafts and games
- usually takes place during the last hour of the school day
- is usually hosted by parents, not by the teacher
- usually occurs three times a year
- can be one heck of a lot of fun

Most classes have three room parties during the school year: Halloween, Winter (Christmas) and Valentine's Day. (And isn't it convenient for room parents that they're each about six weeks apart?) For a lot more information on each of these parties, please see Chapter Three: Specific Room Parties.

☛ Halloween: The Halloween party often kicks off with an out door, round-the-school parade. The parade is so popular that, in case of rain or bad weather, it generally will move indoors. And, of course, the kids will be in their costumes, both for the parade and for your room party. So the party activities need to be gentle; the kids will want to protect their costumes.

☛ Winter: The Winter party takes place on the last day before the winter holiday break. Everyone is so eager to begin vacation that, even though you're all having fun, this can seem like the longest hour of the school year! Be flexible, and have extra games ready.

☛ Valentine's Day: The Valentine's Day party is, of course, scheduled as close as possible to February 14. This may be the easiest party of all because the kids will be opening their valentines, and that eats up time. They'll appreciate games they can play in their seats, because they'll want to read and reread their valentines. And because they're seated, they'll eat a little more than usual.

None of this will happen without the magic ingredient of room parties: room parents. And that's where you come in. How do you become a room parent? There are many ways, depending on the traditions of your child's school:

☛ At many schools, there's an open house within the first few weeks of the school year. There may be a sign-up sheet.

☛ At some schools, you actually sign up to be a room parent a year ahead of time. That is, you may sign up in May, at the end of one school year, to be a room parent for the upcoming school year.

☛ At some schools, the teacher will send home a note with the students. (You don't need me to tell you that sometimes those notes go astray!) One of the grade schools my daughters attended had a weekly newsletter called "The Friday Flier." That was great for keeping up with party dates and calls for volunteers.

☞ At some schools, the teacher may contact a known and trusted parent and ask her or him to round up a team.

DIFFERENT ROLES FOR ROOM PARENTS

Just as there can be many ways for you to sign up, there are many roles you can play:

☞ For each party, there's usually a "head room parent" who is present and is in charge of one of the three basic areas: snacks, crafts or games. The head room parent also makes sure that the other room parents assisting in the classroom are ready to go.

—As head parent, you often can pick which of the three areas (snacks, crafts or games) you want to manage. I prefer games, so I generally reserve that and delegate the other areas. Be nice to yourself; pick the area in which you're most comfortable.

—As head room parent, you may be responsible for creating a team of room parents for a particular party. At best, you'll have a list of dedicated volunteers to call; at worst, you're alone without that handy list. In that case, the teacher no doubt can provide a list of students and parents, and you'll get the privilege of logging a little telephone time.

☞ Remember the old saying that good things come in threes? That's definitely true for room parties: Three parents in the classroom is an ideal number. One way to win a friend for life is to be there to help the head room parent. Maybe he or she will be especially skilled in leading the games; in that case, perhaps you could take the lead on assembling the crafts or on distributing the refreshments.

☞ Don't despair if you simply can't help at the party. I've been a parent who works outside the home, and I know what that does to a schedule. Believe me, you can still help:

—Can you supply some of the materials needed for crafts and send them to school with your child?

—The snacks usually involve drinks, "eats" and paper goods. Paper goods are seasonally decorated paper plates, cups and napkins. Could you help supply those—the napkins, for instance—and send them to school with your child? For a party in my daughter Annie's sixth-grade class, for example, two parents supplied the drinks, another two sent the paper goods, and five provided the eats. And their children delivered it all from home to classroom. That's what I call division of labor!

☛ Here's a tip for a successful room party: Parents who supervise the party shouldn't have to spend any money for supplies—and parents who spend their hard-earned money for supplies shouldn't have to supervise the party. You all need each other, you all help each other and it's all for the benefit of someone you love very much.

I recently heard a story about room parents that's so inspiring I have to share it with you. One class, for good reasons, couldn't field any room parents. In that same school was a class with too many volunteers. Those "extra" room parents took charge in the class that needed some help—even though none of them had children there. No parties were missed, and everyone had a wonderful time. In my book, those volunteers are saints.

My final word on "What is a room party?" Remember: You don't need to spend a lot of time or a lot of money to have a lot of fun.

CHAPTER TWO

Teamwork

A ROOM PARTY NEEDS A LEADER—and maybe that's you—but relax! You won't need to be a "one-man band." A good room party involves a whole orchestra of volunteers. You'll get input and effort from many talented people. A good room party is a partnership, and, fortunately for you, every partner wants to see the party succeed.

If you communicate well with your partners, it will never be "lonely at the top." And who are those partners vital to the success of your room party? Read on...

WORKING WITH THE PRINCIPAL

Over the years as a room parent, you'll deal with many teachers, but the principal often will be the same individual. Principals are important to your room party because they determine the "when, where and how long" of the parties for the entire school. But the teacher is the representative of the school you'll work with most.

Though you probably won't need to work with the principal on your room party, I promise you that he or she has worked hard behind the scenes to help you and your team succeed.

WORKING WITH THE TEACHER

Every teacher, of course, is different. That's exciting, because if you're a room parent for several years, as I hope you will be, you'll have the opportunity to experience a variety of teamwork styles. But despite all those differences, there are some reliable rules of thumb for working with the teacher on a room party:

☛ The room parent should contact the teacher about the upcoming room party, not vice versa. Play it safe, and begin that contact about two weeks before the party.

☛ The teacher will tell you when and where the party will take place and how many students will be participating. Your suggestions will no doubt be welcome—for example, you may have a great idea for a party in the school gym—but, again, the teacher has the final veto on when, where and who.

☛ Teachers should be consulted on everything and have approval of everything. But they should be given no responsibilities before, during or after the party. Why? Because they have their hands full "keeping the lid on" as the party approaches. It becomes harder and harder to teach as excitement for the party builds and becomes a potential distraction. Simply keeping the lid on, as the process of education continues, is more than enough responsibility for that hard-working teacher.

—Despite being so busy, some teachers will want lists of students who are to bring snack and craft supplies to the party. You'll need to create your own system of reminders for students and parents (more on this later), but some teachers will want to help you ensure that all the necessary supplies arrive on time.

—Another area where teachers may go way beyond the call of duty for a room party involves crafts. Some intricate crafts simply can't be done from start to finish during the room party; they need some pre-party class time. If the teacher approves such a craft, you'll need to work out who will supervise those pre-party sessions: a room parent or the teacher.

—Even though you keep the teacher's party responsibilities at an absolute minimum, the teacher will be present at the party. It's a rare teacher who will walk out the door when the party begins. The teacher's degree of participation in the party is strictly up to him or her. He may take a breather in the back of the room—or, especially in the younger grades, she may step down as the authority figure and play games with the kids.

☛ Despite the teacher's reduced responsibilities during the party, he or she is still in charge of the classroom and all the students. Both before and during the party, if the teacher requests that an activity be modified or stopped, you should comply immediately. (In case this sounds a bit ominous, it's a great safety net. If the party gets a little too rambunctious, a good teacher knows how to restore discipline without ruining the fun.)

☛ Despite the occasional temptation to delight the teacher and the students with the unexpected, there should be no surprises for the teacher. Again, you should make it convenient for the teacher to review and approve your party plan, and then, as much as possible, you should stick with that plan.

☛ During the pre-party discussions, the teacher may be able to give you guidance on any religious or dietary situations affecting particular students. In my experience, such matters are rarely a problem. Even at early ages, most kids are well aware of what they can and cannot eat. Occasionally, a parent may send special individual party snacks with a student. And since the party is at the end of the day, if a child, for whatever reason, cannot attend, the inconvenience for his or her parents is minimal.

☛ Teachers are wonderful to work with because, in my experience, they're extremely appreciative of your extra effort. To be blunt, you'd have to do a really lousy job before the teacher would be anything but thankful for your presence. And with all the teamwork and partnership involved in a room party, doing a lousy job is almost impossible!

WORKING WITH ART TEACHERS, PHYSICAL EDUCATION TEACHERS, NURSES AND CUSTODIANS

Art and physical education teachers can be excellent resources for craft and game ideas, but remember that they are busy people. They probably will not be able to attend the party. If you approach these special teachers for help, you may want to write a short note first and follow up with a phone call. That will allow them to pick their own time for brainstorming.

Most room parties won't involve contact with the school nurse or the custodian, but in certain situations, they can help ensure success. The nurse may have suggestions if you have a student with some physical limitations, and the custodian may have advice if you have potentially messy snacks or craft materials or if you need to rearrange the room for games. But in all these situations, your first resource should be the classroom teacher.

Working With Other Room Parents

So who's going to help you with the actual "hands-on" work of the room party? Other room parents, of course, and that's where creating a room party can become a little magical. You'll find people with extraordinary talents who want to help. Maybe you'll discover that your carpool partner is a genius with pipe-cleaners and construction paper. Or maybe your child's best friend's father is a spellbinding storyteller. With some good communication and a little organization, working with other room parents will be one of the best parts of your successful room party. Talk with other room parents. Find out what's worked in the past—and then do it again, maybe with your own spin on it.

How do you find other room parents who are willing to help?

☛ Some schools have a "volunteer sign-up" at an open house early in the year. So there may be a list already waiting for you.

☛ If that list doesn't exist, perhaps you can help create it by distributing, at the beginning of the school year, a volunteer sign-up sheet for all three room parties. This list can allow would-be room parents to specify how they want to help: as "on-site" room parents or as providers of snacks or craft materials.

☛ Your child's teacher can be a good resource in recruitment. Teachers often have a sixth-sense of who the most helpful parents are.

☞ Especially in the lower grades, the kids often are eager to volunteer their parents, though you'll need to confirm that commitment. Right up through fourth grade, the students enjoy having their parents in the classroom. In grades five and six, however, even though your child may be secretly glad to see you, the kids' growing independence means they don't want to be seen needing "mommy and daddy."

☞ Don't forget to ask the dads if they can help. All too often, they're an overlooked resource in room parenting.

☞ As a last resort, you can get a list of your child's classmates and do a little telephone duty. Again, I'm a believer in "Spread the word and spread the work." If you have any acquaintances among the parents in that group, perhaps they can help you with the phone calls.

Chances are excellent that you'll find parents who are willing to help. Most parents will, in some way.

—Finally, don't hesitate to approach parents just because you know that they're busy. They may want to help, and there's a lot of truth in the cliché, "If you really want something done, give it to a busy person."

☞ A recent Parent Teacher Association national survey revealed that the three most cited reasons why parents don't volunteer to help with school activities are:

—Parents do not have enough time

—Parents feel they have nothing to contribute

—Parents don't know how to get involved

As you now know, every parent can contribute to a room party. If their jobs or other commitments prevent them from attending the party, they can supply snacks or craft materials. Most of us want to feel needed and want to believe that we're doing our best for our children. By giving volunteers several options, you'll find that many parents are not only eager to help, but they're also grateful.

☞ Try to give all participating parents at least 10 days

notice. This includes parents who will be in the room with you, parents supplying the snacks and parents supplying craft materials.

—One way to reach party-supply parents is to write notes, take those notes to the classroom, and have the kids take them home. But even though those notes probably do get delivered, you'd be wise to follow them up with a phone call. And, again, sometimes the teacher will want to send his or her own reminders.

☛ Recruiting as many room parents as possible drives down the expenses of crafts and snack materials. Again, my philosophy is that the two or three parents who will actually attend and coordinate the room party should not be asked to buy anything. But the parents who are supplying the materials shouldn't be asked to spend the equivalent of the national debt to feed or entertain 30 hungry, creative kids.

☛ Again, for your own sake, remember to "Spread the word and spread the work." If four parents have signed up to provide food, contact the first on the list and have him or her contact the other three. That's a clear and easy assignment, something for which most of us are grateful.

☛ Should there be a pre-party meeting of parents? That's completely up to you. Some parents enjoy it. I thoroughly enjoyed having meetings with other room parents back when Lucy was in pre-school and Annie was in kindergarten and first grade. But the real appeal was the social element, not the necessity of having a planning meeting. We'd brew a pot of coffee, discuss the party and just have fun. If we hadn't enjoyed getting together so much, we easily could have planned everything over the telephone.

One benefit of those pre-party meetings in the early years was that we all learned whom to call on for future room parties as our kids grew older. The meetings helped us build a network of tried-and-true volunteers who loved the rewards of a successful room party.

☛ Recruiting and working with room parents is usually so easy and so enjoyable that I'll share with you my greatest parent-communication disaster so you can see that even the worst isn't so bad. Somehow one year, not all the parents got contacted about being volunteers. I don't know where the breakdown occurred, but I do know the result. The "left-out" parents were polite, but they were extremely disappointed that they hadn't been able to help. I truly don't want to downplay their disappointment because I know how bad I'd feel, but I hope that new room parents find that disaster reassuring. People weren't upset because they'd been asked to help; they were upset because they weren't asked.

WORKING WITH THE STUDENTS

As eager as all the partners are to create a great room party, no group is more motivated than the students. Getting student input about the party does more than just guarantee that it will be a hit with the kids. That input also creates student ownership of the party, and no owner wants his or her project to go down in flames. An effective safety net for you is to give the students what they want, as much as is realistically possible. Remember: This isn't a party for you (although you'll have a great time). It's a party for the kids.

☛ My husband, Bob, divides children into two categories: spillers and pourers. There's a dramatic turning point in their lives, he says, when they move from spilling their juice to pouring their juice. This gives us a language we can use to show how to get the most out of student input:

—Kids in kindergarten through second grade are spillers.

—Kids in grades three and four are spillers who want to be pourers.

—Kids in grades five and six are pourers who sometimes spill.

GETTING STUDENT INPUT IN KINDERGARTEN
THROUGH SECOND GRADE.

For a parent, these are some of the most precious, thrilling and entertaining years in a child's life. But the fact remains that, at this age, the kids are juice spillers. As much as we love them, we've got to admit that they're not the world's greatest planners. The most useful party input from this group tends to come after the party. If possible, hold a party "postmortem." Find out what they liked best. If you don't want to repeat it exactly at the next party, it still could give you great insight into what rings the bell for this age group.

GETTING STUDENT INPUT IN GRADES THREE AND FOUR

Class surveys before the party seem to work best for this age group. Give them some options with a lot of flexibility, and you'll get both a fun room party and the student ownership that ensures success.

On the other hand, this is the magical age when the spillers have their sights set on becoming pourers. These kids may be ready to form party committees. Basically, that involves three committees: one to select snacks, one to select a craft and one to select games. Or one committee for the entire Halloween party, one for the Winter party and one for the Valentine's Day party. Perhaps the class can be divided into three, and each committee gets to leave the room for a meeting (which is a big thrill for the kids). Of course, a room parent will need to attend each meeting to take notes and, if necessary, to provide a little direction. Is your child's class ready for committees? You probably have a good idea of that, and the teacher, of course, is the world's greatest expert on what the class can handle. But whether it's a survey or the committees, get some student input. At this age, kids will shout "Boring" pretty quickly. With some partnership in the party, however, they'll be shouting "Great!" (or some new slang equivalent!).

Getting Student Input in Grades Five and Six

It's committee time. These are the pourers who only sometimes spill. They're ready for the responsibility of committees (as described above), and you need to be ready for the flurry of innovative ideas that they'll generate. If the lowest-grade parties are the cutest and the middle-grade parties are the most interesting, these are certainly the easiest—if you allow student input. By this age, the students not only want to be partners in the party; they want to be the ruling partners. Of course, you can't have an "anything goes" philosophy, because these students will test the boundaries. But they're more than capable of playing within the rules and developing a party that they'll love. And that makes being a room parent easier than ever.

Call it teamwork or partnership or joint-ownership. Whatever label you use, involving teachers, parents and students in the party means that everyone involved is working toward one goal: the best room party ever. (See why I say a room party means no fears, no tears, just cheers!)

CHAPTER THREE

Specific Room Parties

IN CHAPTER FOUR, we'll discuss the timeline, or the pacing, of a typical room party. But the "room party season" itself has a pace. Again, there traditionally are three major room parties during the school year, and they're spaced about six weeks apart:

- ☞ Halloween: As close to October 31 as possible
- ☞ Winter: Usually in mid to late December
- ☞ Valentine's Day: As close to February 14 as possible.

The purpose of this short chapter is to describe each of the three traditional parties. Knowing the basics of each can help you plan successful snacks, crafts and games. As we discussed in Chapter Two (and as we'll discuss in Chapters Five through Eight), a room party for kindergartners is significantly different from one for sixth graders. But for the moment, we'll concentrate on the basics that apply regardless of the grade level.

One thing that all successful room parties have in common is your good attitude. Be flexible, and have fun. The kids won't think a party is failing unless you signal that it is. If something isn't working as well as you had hoped, laugh it off and move on to Plan B. I've done that many times. During one activity that was more cumbersome than planned, I even asked if any other students wanted to tackle it. None did, and we moved right along. Kids have to follow so many rules during the school day that they can be delighted to see the rules bend a little as a game progresses.

THE HALLOWEEN PARTY

Halloween is often the most popular party of the year, largely because the kids are so proud of their costumes.

- ☞ At many schools, an all-school parade precedes the room parties. This can give room parents more than enough time to set up snacks and prepare for crafts and games. That extra time can be a real confidence booster.

Since this may be your first room party—or at least the first of the school year—having plenty of set-up time lets you prepare for fun.

☛ Snacks are popular at every party, but they're most popular at Halloween. The kids are hungry after the parade, and since the weather during Halloween may still be warm, they can be very thirsty. Be sure to have plenty to drink.

☛ The costumes add a unique element to the Halloween party. The kids are so proud of them that they almost guarantee a great party, but you need to be cautious in your choice of snacks, crafts and games. Be sure to avoid snacks and crafts that are messy. Rough-and-tumble games are also out; they can tear costumes, and some masks or headgear may reduce a child's field of vision. Safety during Halloween games is a vital concern.

☛ "Seat games" can be tough at Halloween because some of the kids may not be able to sit at their desks in costume. I hope some creative room parents out there will prove me wrong, but I've never had much luck with seat games at Halloween parties. Gentle but exciting relays, like the mummy wrap described in Chapter Four, have worked best for me.

The Winter Party

The Winter party celebrates the holiday season. Many of our children are fortunate enough to participate in multicultural classrooms—and a good room party shouldn't favor a particular religious holiday (unless, of course, your child attends a private school with an openly religious affiliation).

☛ If you live in a region that turns into a winter wonderland every December, you know that this party may get canceled because it's simply too hazardous for the children to get to school that day. When the school day itself is canceled, the party often isn't rescheduled because squeezing in all the regular activities at this point in the school year can be so tough for teachers.

—When a Winter party is canceled, families who made food purchases can simply eat the snacks themselves. Or perhaps the food, plus the paper goods and craft supplies, could be donated to a community homeless shelter or a retirement home.

—In case I sound like an alarmist, over one five-year stretch, we had three winter parties canceled. (I live in eastern Kansas, not the North Pole.) On the scheduled day for one winter party, we were hit with eight inches of snow and a high temperature of 15° below.

☛ The Winter party often occurs the last day before winter break, which can make this the hardest party. The kids are charged up about more than just the party; they're also ready to start their vacation. Your safety net could be some extra games, just in case they whirl through all the scheduled activities at record speed. Have both extra seat games and extra relays. The games portion of the party is the easiest one to extend.

☛ The snacks can be fairly simple because at this time of year, many families are planning their own exciting menus.

THE VALENTINE'S DAY PARTY

Though the Valentine's Day party is in the heart of winter, a "no school/snow day" usually doesn't mean a canceled party. The schedule now may be flexible enough that the party is simply postponed, not canceled.

☛ This may be the easiest party of the three, because the kids will be absorbed in opening their valentines and comparing notes with their friends. The valentines themselves provide the major portion of the entertainment.

☛ In every grade—kindergarten through sixth—the opening of valentines may take some time. This, again,

means that they're at their desks for awhile. And that means that they'll eat a little more, probably, than they did at the Winter party.

☛ Even though desktops may be cluttered with valentines and valentines boxes, seat games are popular and work well because the kids want to stay with their valentines. (Often, they've had the valentines all day but haven't been able to open them or touch them.) If you schedule a relay game, it might be best to make it short and save it for the very end.

☛ If you schedule a craft (I think the valentines themselves, along with the valentines boxes, are the craft), it probably should be simple. Students aren't as protective of their valentines as they are of their Halloween costumes, but they're still careful with them.

INNOVATIONS AND OTHER ROOM PARTIES

By now I hope you're asking, "Are we limited to just three room parties?" I'd say, "Of course not—but you'd better check with the teacher."
Or you may be asking, "What's this fascination with seat games and in-room relays?" Half the fun of the room party is the creativity. One of my great hopes in writing this book is that you'll write back with super ideas that never occurred to me.

Here's one slight innovation that I've used with success. If your child is, say, a fifth grader in a school with three fifth grades, why not have a combined class party in the school gym. Kids enjoy breaking out of the school routine, and this innovation is bound to do that.
Despite all the differences in the three basic room parties, there are important similarities: You're going to have a great time, and there's going to be at least one smiling youngster in that classroom who's very proud to be your child.

CHAPTER FOUR

Room Party Timelines

THE CLOCK HAS STARTED. Thirty young faces, eyes shining, turn to you, waiting for the magic to begin.
And you're equal to the task.
Why?
Because you have a plan with a timeline.

Who was it who said, "The readiness is all"? Hamlet? He would have been a great room parent, because "readiness" in a room party means fun, success and relaxation. Remember our goal: No fears, no tears, just cheers!

Though room parties vary with the occasion, successful parties have a definite pace. That's what this chapter is about: helping you establish the pace—the timeline—of a room party that's fun and rewarding for everyone.

ROOM PARTY TIMELINES: THE BASICS

Room parties usually last one hour, and they move from low-energy to high-energy activities. (Of course, "low-energy" is a relative term with excited grade schoolers.) The room party generally has five separate sections:

- ☛ The set-up
- ☛ The snacks
- ☛ The craft
- ☛ The games
- ☛ The clean-up

These five sections occur in four 15-minute periods:

- ☛ The first 15 minutes
- —The set-up
- —The snacks
- ☛ The second 15 minutes
- —The snacks continue
- —The craft
- ☛ The third 15 minutes
- —The craft continues
- —Seat games (games that kids can play at their desks, as snacks and crafts are finished)

☛ The fourth 15 minutes
—Relay games
—Clean-up

The first 15 minutes and the last 15 minutes are pretty well established, but there can be a lot of flexibility during that middle half hour. For example, you may have a party in which the snacks are so intricate that you really don't want a craft. Or you may want to ask if the kids are ready to move from snacks to a craft or a seat game. The older kids may say, "No, we want to sit and talk." But trust me: You won't have to ask the younger kids twice. They're ready to play.

So this four-period schedule is meant to be a guideline only, not a rigid rule. Please don't feel that you have to be a clock-watcher. Be flexible and have a great time! One hint: Sometimes things go so quickly that you get ahead of your timetable. Be prepared with extra games to fill any unbudgeted time at the end. (More on this later.)

THE SET-UP
Don't be late!

Please forgive my bluntness, but schools run like clock-work, and the school day will proceed on its own schedule, not yours.

So how soon should you arrive in order to set up the room party? As always, consult the teacher. But in most cases, 15 minutes early will be more than enough. Sometimes, the class may have a 15-minute recess right before the party. That should allow you plenty of time to set up the snacks.

Halloween set-ups are easy. You can prepare while the kids are marching in their traditional Halloween parade. One year during the parade, we had time to set out the refreshments and build a giant spider web made of yarn in the classroom. When the kids returned, each had to grab a strand of yarn and trace it to its source. I don't know who had more fun: the web-builders or the web-unravelers. (As fun as it was, the spider web game was an exception for me; I prefer set-ups that one room parent can create, just in case other room parents have to cancel at the last moment.)

If there's not a recess or a Halloween parade, chances are strong that the teacher won't want to see you until the scheduled beginning of the party. The moment you walk into the classroom, the students are going to know who you are and why you're there. If you have all your supplies and you're prepared, five minutes is more than enough to set up a traditional room party.

The transition from class time to party time is easy. Often, the teacher will make the announcement and have the kids clear their desktops. In my experience, the teacher is usually so appreciative you're managing the party that he or she will help ensure that desktops are cleared, that you have a table for snacks and that the room is rearranged, if need be, for any relay games.

THE SNACKS

Beginning the party with snacks makes you an instant hero to the class. Grade-school kids are eating machines, and the usually forbidden pleasure of food and drinks in the classroom thrills them. Starting with the snacks provides a can't-miss beginning for your party.

Another good reason to start with the snacks involves parents' budgets. You'll probably be setting out chips, cookies, candy, ice cream, soft drinks—naturally, the most expensive things in the grocery store. If, for any reason, the party gets cut short or you run out of time, you don't want to waste the food, drinks and paper goods. Parents who can't come to the party but are supplying the refreshments are important contributors. You don't want to hurt their feelings by sending the food home.

THE CRAFT

I think that you can have a perfectly good room party without a craft—just devote that extra time to food and games. But some room parents I've worked with can make crafts a magical experience. If you have a craft, there are basically two schedules it can follow:

☛ It can be made during the room party; or

☛ It can be made before the party during an earlier class. If this is the case, often some finishing touch is added during the room party:

—for example, the room parent leading the craft may bring an essential ingredient to complete it

—or perhaps a project is finally dry, and students can hold it for the first time

—or maybe the thrill of the craft is allowing each child to show off his or her handiwork.

In the case of a valentines box, often completed before the party, just using the box to hold valentines from classmates is the thrill.

Crafts made before the party require good communication and cooperation with the teacher and, perhaps, with the art teacher.

Sometimes a room parent may be asked to help with those pre-party crafts. If the room parents and the teacher opt for a craft made during the party, be sure to remember how quickly the hour will go. Crafts can be time-intensive, especially if they involve gluing or painting or anything else that needs to dry. A good craft can be a smash hit at a room party, but it probably shouldn't infringe on the time set aside for snacks and games. An intricate craft at Halloween, for example, when the kids are so involved with their costumes, may be too much. And a paint or glue spill on a costume can be a disaster.

If you've found a craft that you know the kids will love, be sure to try it out at home first with your own child and some of his or her friends. How long does it take them? Did they like it? What questions did they ask? How big a mess did they make?

In case I sound too skeptical about crafts, one of the best room parties I ever helped sponsor involved using the food as a craft. We made sundaes in a fifth-grade Valentine's Day party, and the making was as much fun as the eating. Here's how it worked:

☞ Two days before the party, I attended the class and asked what toppings they would put on an ice-cream sundae. Ice-cream flavors weren't an option, I told them; we were going with vanilla. In a class of 30 students, we ended up with 15 toppings. (You wouldn't believe what some of the suggestions were, but the kids had a great time.) Note here that we involved the students in the planning of the party. Teamwork helps ensure success.

☞ I asked whoever suggested a topping if he or she could bring a little of that topping to the party. Not much was needed, I stressed, since we had 15 toppings.

☞ Before visiting the class, I had signed up parents to supply the ice cream. If one of their children suggested a topping, we found another volunteer to bring it. No room parents had to be double dippers.

☞ The day before the party, the "supplier" children got a reminder note to take home to their parents. (There are never too many reminders for something like this. Often, you'll be lucky and the teacher will help. If possible, give the teacher a list of suppliers.)

☞ At the party, we had a "sundae bar." Every child started out with one scoop and one frantic trip through a bizarre collection of toppings. After that, it was a free-for-all. First come, first served.

☞ The kids ate their sundaes, opened valentines, revisited the sundae bar, discussed valentines… We didn't even have any games. We couldn't tear them away from their desks.

☛ By the way, this smorgasbord technique can certainly be used for snacks other than sundaes—cookie decoration, for example.

But were the sundaes really crafts? You bet! You should have seen some of the ice-cream sculptures those kids concocted. If a craft is supposed to draw out a child's imagination and creative energy, all with a little bit of discipline, then these sundaes were masterpieces.

There's an interesting sequel to the sundae story. We had leftover toppings galore, and, at the final bell, the kids vanished with their valentines. I thought, "Uh oh, these aren't coming to my house." I can inhale half a bag of candy and not even think twice.

Later that week, the three fifth grade classes at my daughters' grade school were going ice skating at a rink in a nearby city. So we kept the leftover toppings, asked the two other fifth grade classes to supply popular brands of dry cereals and made "trail mix." We combined everything in an enormous bowl, volunteers from each class scooped equal amounts into sandwich bags, and *voila!* A snack for the ice-skating field trip.

I guess the moral here is that a good craft can keep on giving. Finally, you may be asking, "If crafts can be time intensive, why not do them last? Then if you run out of time, no great problem. Right?"

Wrong. Crafts come second—after snacks but before the games—for two good reasons:

☛ Like the snacks, crafts can involve a small expenditure on the parents' part. And that should not go to waste.

☛ Crafts usually aren't a high-energy activity. You wouldn't want to go from snacks, a low-energy activity, to games, a high-energy activity—and then back to low-energy with crafts. The kids would simply be too wound up. As I said earlier, I'm not the world's "craftiest" room parent. But I've worked with room parents who are geniuses, and I know that a good craft can captivate young imaginations. I hope that you'll write me with your craft success stories.

THE GAMES

Let the games begin!

The party is entering the home stretch, and it's time to find an outlet for all that youthful energy. Games are limited only by the imagination, but for room parties, two types can be useful: seat games and relays. Seat games usually come first and build up to the relays.

☛ Seat games are just that: games that the kids can play while still seated at their desks. This can be essential when they're at various stages of finishing snacks and crafts. Seat games can be high-energy, but not as high as relay games, which are the peak of the party. These also can be "floor games" if desktops are too crowded with Halloween costume parts or valentines:

☛ Relay games involve dividing the class into teams. The teams then compete against one another in completing some task, and the first team done wins. Relays may involve moving some desks, so, of course, teacher approval is needed before the room party.

At a sixth-grade Halloween party, for example, our relay was a "mummy wrap" in which teams of three students competed to see who could first wrap their designated mummies from tip to toe in toilet paper (don't blame me; the kids requested it). They had a wonderful time but were too fast: We still had about five minutes left. What to do? The room parents went to Plan B: our extra relay. The class formed four lines. Each took a roll of toilet paper and did an "over and under." That is, the first person passed the roll over his shoulder to the next person in line, who passed it between her legs to someone who passed it over his shoulder… When the roll got to the end of the line, it had to come back forward the same way. And of course

you couldn't break the string of paper. Sounds crazy, I know, but it was a lot of fun. And the students never knew that it was part of a back-up plan.

Even though there's usually time for only two relays, I always try to prepare five, just in case we get ahead of schedule. If that sounds like too much work, it's really not. Usually, my extras are just variations on the scheduled relays.

When should the games end? Get the teacher's guidance on that well before the party. The teacher probably will want a bit of time with the students at the very end of the school day. When the games are over, the teacher usually will reassume command. Desktops will be cleared, homework reminders will be issued and the class will be dismissed. (Remember that as indispensable as you are, it's still the teacher's classroom. During the party, he or she may be in the background or, even better, enjoying the activities with the students—but have no doubts about who the boss is. Most teachers are thrilled to relinquish control for an hour, but before the students go home, the school day may need some closure that only a teacher can provide.)

THE CLEAN-UP

Yes, this is the responsibility of the room parents. And you'll probably enjoy it because it gives you time to pat each other on the back for sponsoring a great room party. Unless you hear differently from the teacher, the goal is to put the room back in shape. Again, the teacher may step in at the end of the party to help you ensure that desktops are returned to order.

If snacks or other supplies are left over, do your best to return them, via the students, to the parents who purchased them. If that's not possible, perhaps you can offer them to the teacher. And if that doesn't work, I hope you've got great will power because a lot of those snacks are great, and none are low calorie.

CHAPTER FIVE

Snacks, Crafts and Games: An Introduction

LET'S BEGIN WITH A CONFESSION:

Here is what these final chapters are not:

☛ These final chapters do not contain 1,001 Whiz-Bang Ideas for Snacks, Crafts and Games. I am going to share with you some sure-fire ideas that have never let me down, but there are better books than mine for snacks, crafts and game ideas.

Here's what these final chapters are:

☛ These final chapters offer guidelines on how to hit home runs with your snacks, crafts and games. And, again, I couldn't resist including just a few of my favorite kid pleasers.

This introductory chapter on snacks, crafts and games contains general advice that I've found to be true for kindergarten through sixth grade. The next three chapters, however, get more specific, offering advice for children in these age groups:

☛ Kindergarten through second grade

☛ Third and fourth grades

☛ Fifth and sixth grades

No matter what age your grade-schooler is, some general guidelines for snacks, crafts and games always hold true:

☛ Plug into the school "grapevine." Which parents are good at what tasks? For instance, who are the ultimate crafts masters? Even if those parents aren't in your child's class, they still may be flattered and very helpful if you call and ask for advice. If they are in your child's class, maybe they'll volunteer for crafts.

☛ Ask your child and his or her friends what they like to do for room parties. And consider using those children to do some pre-party testing of your (or their) ideas.

☛ If a particular idea was a hit at a previous room party, consider using it again. That last party was more than a month ago—and as you know all too well, kids will repeat their favorite experiences again and again. (How many

times, for example, did your pre-schooler crawl up into your lap with that tattered, favorite book? I'll bet you had it memorized.)

☞ Remember that everything—even old favorites—can be modified, improved and adapted to new circumstances, such as a Halloween game changed to suit Valentine's Day.

☞ And one final bit of general philosophy. I hope this book is just your starting point. I'd be thrilled if you took my ideas and improved them for your own room parties. (And I'd be even more thrilled if you wrote and told me of your successes. We're all in this together, and we can learn from each other.)

GENERAL ADVICE ON SNACKS

Snacks come first as the party begins with fairly low-energy activities.

☞ Snack providers don't need to attend the party. Parents who have unavoidable time conflicts may want to volunteer in this area. Don't hesitate to point this out if you're recruiting volunteers. You'll find parents who want to help and want to feel needed—and snacks may be the perfect solution for them.

☞ One Halloween snack strategy that works wonders in every grade, kindergarten through sixth, is dry ice. Just plop it into some punch, and *voila!* Instant Witch's Brew. For the younger kids, this can be a great backdrop for a room parent who stages a dramatic reading of a creepy Halloween story.

GENERAL ADVICE ON CRAFTS

OK, I'll say it again. Crafts are not my greatest strength; I'm a games person. I have unending respect for "crafty" parents. If you are one, please volunteer the great gift that you have. Someone like me (not to mention the kids) will bless you.

☛ Crafts tend to attract fewer volunteers than snacks—but more volunteers than games. Again, if you're recruiting volunteers, plug in to your school grapevine and find out who can do what.

☛ Teachers can be a fabulous resource for crafts (but don't ask them to do the craft during the party). They may have ideas that would supplement their teaching, or they may offer advice on what tickled the kids last year. In all three areas—snacks, crafts and games—communication with the teacher is essential. But it's most important in the area of crafts.

☛ Halloween crafts should be simple and clean. You don't want paint or glue to damage a Halloween costume.

☛ Remember that crafts can't be too intricate or too time-consuming to be completed in a short time. As I noted in "Chapter Four: Room Party Timelines," there are basically two schedules for crafts:

—They can be made during the room party; or

—They can be made before the party—during an earlier class, for example. Then add some finishing touches during the party.

☛ Recall that crafts are a medium-energy activity, coming after snacks but before games. Sometimes a "non-traditional" activity instead of a craft works well at this point in the party—maybe a story, instead of a craft, especially if that story is a spooky Halloween story presented by a room parent dressed in costume. The lights are out, a flashlight casts creepy shadows, the dry ice bubbles away in the punch bowl… You get the picture. A story like this, of course, works better for the lower grades than the upper. In the higher grades, maybe you can begin the story but then, at a key point, hand the flashlight to one of the students and let her continue.

☛ Another alternative is to get crafty parents together before the party and make a "party favor" for each child and perhaps for the teacher, too. For example, for the Winter party, maybe room parents could make fabric snowmen that can fit over a doorknob. Some super room parents have twice done this for my daughters' room parties, and Annie and Lucy were thrilled. One of the favors was for a fifth grade party, so this isn't limited to just the lower grades.

GENERAL ADVICE ON GAMES

Although I love room parties from start to finish, for me, here's where the real fun starts: with the games.

☛ Ideally, games involve and entertain the entire class, and you already know what a wonderful variety of kids that means. I've learned to be sensitive, I hope, in the kinds of games I select. For example, no competitive balloon popping during my parties (where the kids pop a balloon by sitting on it). That can be embarrassing for both the heavy and the thin children.

☛ Even though the games should be designed to involve and entertain the entire class, don't force anyone to play. Decisions like that belong to the teacher. On those very few occasions when I've had a student who, for whatever reason, chose not to participate, it only took a few minutes of the first game before he or she had a sudden change of heart.

☛ If a particular game was a roaring success at an earlier party, do it again. Maybe put a new spin on it, but don't worry about straight repetition. The kids will greet it like a beloved old friend. I've done that silly "over and under" toilet paper game about 10 times. In fact, one year the students insisted that we do it at all three parties.

☛ For a real adventure for the kids, you may want to consider approaching the school's physical education teacher to see about reserving the gym for the games—or for the whole party. The kids' school days often are so regimented that any break in the routine can be a thrill for them.

☛ Games can and should be challenging, but they shouldn't be complicated. Remember that time is short and expectations are high. Avoid games requiring detailed detailed instructions.

☛ Basically, there are two types of games: seat (or quiet) games and relays. Many room parties include both kinds.

—Seat games are just that: The students usually are in their seats or, perhaps, sitting on the floor in a clear area. Often, these are individual, not team, games, but by sitting together, students can form teams for seat games. Seat games usually come before relays because they're not as high-energy an activity as relay games are.

On Halloween and Valentine's Day, when desktops can be crowded, you may want to consider a floor game—or, at least, a seat game that doesn't involve the desktop.

—Relay games are usually the last activity of the party. They involve dividing the class into teams and giving them some kind of competitive game to perform. Gentle warning: Here's where the fun, the frenzy and the energy usually peak.

☛ Seat games may not be necessary for Valentine's Day parties, when time will be spent opening the valentines and laughing and screaming and maybe even blushing. But have some seat games ready just in case, especially for the lower grades. The younger kids don't seem to pause over and savor their cards as much as the older ones do.

☛ If a seat game involves paper and pencil, such as word jumbles, consider dividing the class into small teams. During real tests, students aren't allowed to speak with each other, of course, so being able to talk and work with others during a room party "quiz" has the lure of the forbidden.

☛ Games are the greatest area of flexibility in the party. If you're ahead of schedule, play some extra seat games or relays to eat up that time. If you're behind schedule, maybe skip the seat game and go straight to the relay.

☛ Usually, there will be time for about two relays, but I always have five ready, just in case we get to the games ahead of schedule. This doesn't mean that you need five separate relays prepared. Instead, you can have variations on a relay that the kids just played. For example, if a relay game somehow involves walking forward, make them do it again—walking backward.

During one party when we were far ahead of schedule, one of the relays involved a Ping-Pong ball. We had plenty of time for another relay, so when the Ping-Pong-ball relay ended, I borrowed the teacher's masking tape, made two long parallel tape-lines on the floor about four feet apart, had the kids stretch out on the floor, and there we had it: Ping-Pong soccer. I put the ball between the two lines, and the two teams began to huff and puff, trying to blow the ball over the other team's line. Sounds goofy, I know, but it was a big hit.

☛ How many teams do you need for a relay? It all depends, but usually just two is fine.

☛ Students usually can form their own teams, but it can be a good idea to consult the teacher beforehand. Some students may need to be separated, and some may need to be paired. The teacher, of course, will have insight on this.

☛ There may be rare situations when team competition isn't a good idea. For example, if a class has some kind of unfortunate split in it and students already are divided into two camps, teams may be a bad idea. If they form their own teams, the split will appear, and if you form the teams, they may be unhappy with their teammates. In a rare case like this, you may want to use a game where the entire class works as a team to win. Balloon volleyball is a good example. Simply get the kids in their seats, bat four or five balloons into the air and see how long the kids can keep batting them up before they touch the floor. Balloon volleyball works best in grades two through six. Before that, the kids just don't have the coordination.

☛ Whether you create the teams or you allow the students to create them, be on the watch for kids who get left out. Again, the teacher may have some advice for you on who the loners are. I've found it easy and effective to steer a child to one of the teams and say, "Johnny (or Mary) will be joining your team." Then, before there's any questioning, I quickly address all the students and begin the game. Who wants to argue over a teammate when you can be playing the game instead?

☛ Finally, a personal point, but it's one I feel strongly about. I work hard to avoid games where there are clear and visible losers. For that reason, I never use "Musical Chairs" during a room party. I don't avoid competition, but I do avoid games that shine a spotlight on one lone loser. A big advantage of team games is that, usually, no one child feels responsible for a loss. Whatever games you choose, however, a fast pace will keep anyone from dwelling on anything but the task at hand.

Before we move into the chapters on snacks, crafts and games for the different age groups, let me offer a small loophole. The ideas I suggest for the different age groups are based on my experience. Your child may be in an incredible first grade that's ready for one of the ideas I list for third and fourth graders. In other words, be realistic, but aim high!

CHAPTER SIX

Snacks, Crafts and Games: Kindergarten Through Second Grade

REMEMBER THOSE OLD NURSERY RHYMES about "snips and snails and puppy dog tails" and "sugar and spice and everything nice"? That's what little boys and girls supposedly were made of. Well, what are kindergartners, first graders and second graders made of?

☛ Endless energy and curiosity. Despite all that energy, these kids will be slow eaters during the snacks.

☛ Weak group skills in the younger kids. If you have relay games, you'll need a lot of adult supervision. By second grade, however, you'll see great development in this area.

☛ Good basic muscle control, but the younger kids won't have detailed coordination yet. Again, that will change dramatically as they move from first to second grade. By the time of the second-grade Valentine's Day party, they'll be able to handle any relay you throw at them.

☛ Occasional bickering and tattle-taling. Don't worry; it's normal at this age.

☛ Increasing competitive drive in the older kids in this group.

Good relays will be wildly popular in second-grade parties. Recruiting room parents is easier during kindergarten through second grade than for parties in upper grades. Children are launched on the adventure of school, and the parents want to be a part of it. Parents actually can get their feelings hurt if they want to help but aren't called. So if you're in charge, please try to use every volunteer. Trust me: In this age group, you'll want all the help you can get, more than you'll need for the older kids. But if you're knee-deep in eager room parents, perhaps you can divide them among the three parties.

SNACK ADVICE

Simplicity is the key at this age. As you well know, young children want to understand what they're eating. At home, they may challenge your patience as they analyze your best casserole, searching doubtfully for something that looks familiar.

☞ By and large, kids this age love sugar, as opposed to the salty snacks that appeal to sixth graders. And for once, that's where my advice stops. Should you serve them sugar-based foods or something healthier? It's your call. Do remember, though, that it is a party, and it's their party.

☞ These kids also love the seasonal paper goods: the Halloween napkins, the winter-scene cups, the Valentine's Day paper plates (the older kids couldn't care less). That's the bad news because those items are expensive. The good news is that these children won't eat as much as older students. The money saved on food can go toward paper goods.

☞ You can also buy less food for this group than you would for older students. Kids this age will dawdle over their food, taking longer to eat it and eating less.

☞ Remember earlier when I told you that my husband, Bob, divides kids into two groups: spillers and pourers? Well, these are the spillers. Don't serve them drinks until they're seated. And when they want a refill, have them place their cups on their desktops. If Billy is holding his cup as you pour and Susie calls him, he's going to turn his whole body, cup and all—and you'll be irrigating his desktop. Get the cup on the desktop and help him hold it as you pour.

My suggestions

☞ Halloween: Doughnut holes with cider or orange drink. And don't forget the dry ice for the punchbowl.

☞ Winter party: Baked cookies (snowmen, boots, snowflakes) for the kids to decorate with frosting, sprinkles, etc.

☞ Valentine's Day: Ice-cream cone cupcakes. Just pour standard cake mix into a flat-bottomed ice-cream cone. Fill to within one inch of the top. Bake at 350° for 20-25 minutes. Frost and decorate.

Note: Parents may be very particular about what kinds of drinks they want children of this age to have.

CRAFTS ADVICE

At this age, crafts can be very simple gifts for Mom and Dad. The kids will be proud, and the parents, of course, will melt.

☞ School art teachers can be superb resources for quick and easy crafts for young children. They know exactly what materials the students can best work with. Again, however, be sure to use those teachers just to brainstorm as sources of ideas. Room parents need to do the actual work in the classroom.

☞ The party favors mentioned in the previous chapter work particularly well at this age if for, whatever reason, you decide not to do a craft at your room party. I know some room parents who will get together before a party, and put together 30 party favors as they chat. Some of my best friendships have begun as I planned a room party with "strangers."

MY SUGGESTIONS

☞ Halloween: Make a ghost! Cover a sucker with a white facial tissue. Wrap a white pipe cleaner around the neck and twist it to make arms. Add eyes with a black marker.

☞ Winter party: Often, the cookie decoration described above under the snacks will function as a craft. But don't hesitate to develop something new and wonderful.

☞ Valentine's Day: Create a bunny from three valentines. Cut a large heart (4 inches high) from pink paper. Cut two smaller hearts, one for feet and one for ears. Add a cotton tail with glue. You may want to cut the hearts first and do the gluing.

GAMES ADVICE

There's a huge gulf between the physical abilities of a kindergartner and those of a second grader. Giving a kindergartner a pencil and a maze is a sure recipe for frustration. But a second grader will be eager to show off his or her growing coordination.

☛ Physical education teachers can be a great source of ideas for you. More than anyone else, perhaps, they know what the physical abilities of the kids are. But, just as with the art teachers, don't draft them to do the work. That's the job of the room parent, and you won't want to surrender it to anyone else.

☛ Have an excess of volunteers? Ask them to help monitor the games, especially the relays, which can border on out-of-control. (Don't worry; the fun exceeds the chaos every time.)

☛ The first and second graders love secrets. Guessing games can be popular seat games.

☛ Again, consider reading a story instead of having a seat game or, perhaps, instead of having a craft. Kindergartners especially love to have books read to them.

My SUGGESTIONS

☛ Halloween seat game: Tell or read a spooky story, with mood music, lights out, your own costume, a flashlight under your chin, dry ice bubbling in the punchbowl—and whatever other creepy trappings you can think of.

☛ Halloween relay: The Broom Zoom - Kids ride a broom to a point and back again and then hand it to the next person. If that's too easy, make them do half the trip riding backward.

☛ Winter party seat game: Where's My Reindeer? - The kids sit in a circle. One is Santa, who stands in the middle and, with eyes closed, is gently spun around by a room parent. Santa then points at one child, who leaves the room. Santa then opens his or her eyes and guesses which "reindeer" is missing.

☛ Winter party relay: Goin' on a Trip: Divide the class into two teams. Have two old suitcases with easy-to-put-on old clothes in them (maybe some huge galoshes and an old

hat). Each child runs to his or her team's suitcase, opens it, puts on the clothes, takes them off, and then runs back and tags a teammate.

☛ Valentine's Day seat game: It's unlikely that you'll need one. Opening the valentines usually means that you'll go straight to the relays, which the kids won't want to miss.

☛ Valentine's Day relay: Whose Shoe? Divide the class into boys and girls. One group leaves the room. Each member of the remaining group removes a shoe and places it in the center of the room. The absent group returns, each member selects a shoe and then tries to find the owner.

CHAPTER SEVEN

Snacks, Crafts and Games: Third and Fourth Grades

MY FAVORITE ROOM PARTIES have been in third and fourth grades. They can get pretty wild, but everyone has a great time. These kids are the spillers who want to be pourers, and they are endlessly interesting as they push their limits. What are the basic characteristics of third and fourth graders?

☛ You'll notice the beginning of girl/boy divisions, even in the formation of teams. The kids are starting to notice the opposite sex, even if that notice seems based mostly on contempt.

☛ The love of secrets that you saw in second graders has blossomed into a love of puzzles, codes and mysteries. Word games can be great seat games at this age. In general, seat games can be a lot more complicated than those for the younger kids.

☛ There's the beginning of serious respect for the rules. Don't be surprised by occasional charges of "Hey, you cheated! You stepped over the line." Be ready to referee the situation and quickly move on.

☛ The kids are much more coordinated than first and second graders, and they're willing to tackle challenging relays, such as three-legged races, if you can go outdoors or use the gym.

☛ As they seek responsibility, they may be ready for party committees. The teacher can help you judge whether they can handle the planning of their own parties. My experience is that third and especially fourth graders will tell you what they want to eat and what they want to play, but they often draw a blank on crafts suggestions.

It can be a little harder to attract room-parent volunteers for this age group compared with parties for the younger kids. And that's natural. Some parents want to move on to other things. Others believe that the growing independence their child is seeking means that they're not needed and that they should step back a little to nurture that independence.

I know how busy those reluctant parents are; I've been there. But I urge you and all the potential room parents you speak with not to miss the third and fourth grade parties. I really don't know why, but these are the most intense parties in grade school. The kids in every grade have fun, but no one in the world has more fun than third and fourth graders who are determined to enjoy themselves. You'll get caught up in the spirit, and by the end of the party, you'll not only be a hero to 30 panting kids, but you'll also be on top of the world yourself. It's a great feeling.

One minor caution: With this age group, notes to parents often don't make it home. Don't ignore that avenue to other room parents, but don't let it be your only channel to them. I get on the phone a lot, which isn't a problem because the calls can be so quick.

SNACKS ADVICE

Third and fourth graders will eat more than the younger kids—in fact, you'll see them inhale the food—so if you're an old hand at parties for younger kids, plan on increasing the supplies.

☛ If the teacher thinks it's a good idea, set up a student snacks committee. The kids know what they want to eat, and it gives them some ownership of the party. And that makes them determined to have fun.

☛ As kids get older, they tend to move away from the sweet snacks and toward the salty ones. You may notice that in this age group.

☛ Again, these are the kids who want to be pourers, but they're still spillers. When filling and refilling, don't let them hold their cups up to you. Get each cup placed firmly in the middle of the desktop. Hold it with one hand and pour with the other.

MY SUGGESTIONS

☛ Halloween: Cookie Monsters—Bake or buy plain sugar cookies. Bring green frosting for a face, chocolate sprinkles or strings of licorice for hair, small marshmallows for eyes, blue food coloring for dots on the eyes (use a cotton swab), candy corn for the nose, and red hots for the mouth. Kids get so caught up in this that the cookies can become the Halloween craft as well.

☛ Winter Party: Corn Flake Wreaths—These are made using the recipe for crisp rice bars, but use corn flakes instead, and add green food coloring to the melted marshmallows. Place on the pan in the shape of little wreaths, and, while still warm, add red hots. Later, bows can be added with tube frosting, if you'd like.

☛ Valentine's Day: Try a repeat of Cookie Monsters, perhaps with the little candy hearts as added decorations. Remember: If it worked well before, chances are strong that the kids will be delighted to see it again. And that surely makes your job easier.

CRAFTS ADVICE

Games are so popular with third and fourth graders that crafts tend to get squeezed out. Perhaps, in conjunction with the teacher or the art teacher, you could have the kids start the craft several days before the party, and just the finishing touch would be added during the party. Or recall that if the snacks involve a lot of creative decorating, as the Cookie Monsters do, they can also function as crafts.

MY SUGGESTIONS

☛ Halloween: The Cookie Monster snack can be a craft. Or you might consider making ghosts with cotton balls, white paint and black paper. Simply dab the cotton balls into the paint and then onto the paper to make a whole troop of ghosts.

☛ Winter party: The most popular room party craft ever for my daughters was a "party favor" that Annie received in the second grade. It was a Christmas tree that fits over a doorknob—and, believe me, Christmas still doesn't start in our home until that treasure is located and placed on our front door. If you want to avoid the religious connotations of a Christmas tree, how about a snowman? The kids didn't make the doorknob hangers during the party. Instead, some inspired room parents made them before the party and distributed them during the crafts period.

☛ Valentine's Day: Again, the cookies can be a craft. Another idea is a worm pencil (sorry to go from cookies to worms!). For each child you'll need a red pencil, three small red pom-pom balls, three small white pom-pom balls, antennas, eyes and glue. Glue everything onto the pencil, and there's one cute worm. You can get all of these inexpensive parts at a crafts store.

GAMES ADVICE

Again, this is the big category for this age group, more popular, usually, than even the snacks. Have extra games ready just in case the kids are so energized that they charge ahead of your schedule.

☛ I think one reason I love third and fourth grade parties so much is that the kids are flexing their muscles in so many ways. They're ready for challenging seat games, and they're eager for some fairly difficult and competitive relays. (But as always, make sure that the games are clear and easy to explain. These kids are ready to party; they don't want long explanations.)

☛ The games are so important for these particular parties that, again, a party committee in which the kids choose their own games can be a great idea. As always, this committee needs to meet well before the party.

MY FAVORITES

☞ Halloween seat game: Guesstimate—Fill a jar with candy corn and let each child guess how many pieces there are. They can write down their guesses and place them in a second empty jar. You can add mystery by responding to each guess: "A little low…a little high…oh, that's the closest so far…" By the way, don't give all the candy to the winner!

☞ Halloween relay: Spoon race—This keeps the kids moving slowly, which protects their costumes. Basically, form two teams, place some Halloween candy in two spoons, and have each child move his or her team's spoon to a certain point in the room and then return it, handing it off to a teammate. Or the kids can dump the candy into a bowl and quickly return to hand off the spoon. If that's the case, have a room parent ready with each team to reload the spoon with candy. If this moves too quickly, substitute a cotton ball for the candy and do it again.

☞ Winter party seat game: Winter Bingo—This is played just like Tic-Tac-Toe, but the game card will be larger. Draw a bingo card with 25 squares in it and with a free spot in the center. Photocopy it, and give each child a blank card. Then write several winter words on the chalkboard—for example, ice, cold, snow, Santa, etc. Let the kids fill in their cards, one letter per square, with whichever of those words they want. Thus, no two cards will be the same. Then you call out individual letters from your winter words, and wait until someone scores a bingo. If that goes too quickly, or if you want to make it more difficult, announce that only diagonal bingos will count.

☞ Winter relay: Nose Push—As usual, divide into two teams. Kids use their noses to push a Ping-Pong ball to a designated point. They then pick it up and run it back to a teammate.

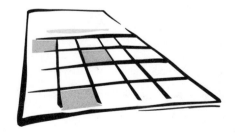

☛ Valentine's Day seat game: Because of the time devoted to opening valentines, there may not be time for a seat game. If there is, you may want to be ready with a Valentine's Day variation of Winter Bingo, the Winter party seat game.

☛ Valentine's Day relay: Heart Break—Members of the two teams must place a small red heart between their knees and run to a designated spot and back again before handing the heart to the next teammate. Whoever drops the heart may continue, but he or she now has a broken heart (and may be the recipient of some gentle, flattering teasing on your part).

CHAPTER EIGHT

Snacks, Crafts and Games: Fifth and Sixth Grades

FIFTH AND SIXTH GRADERS may be your toughest customers, but relax! These can be the easiest parties of all. Why? Because you've formed party committees, and the kids have made the decisions. They've picked all their favorites, and they're sure to enjoy the party they've designed. Besides a willingness and ability to assume some control, what else characterizes fifth and sixth graders?

☛ They're not only increasingly critical of others, they're increasingly critical of themselves and their own work. That's one reason I downplay crafts in these parties.

☛ They'll grab any chance they can to push the limits and test the boundaries, so how about some safe activities that still seem wildly out of place in a classroom?

☛ They've become intensely conscious of their bodies. Three-legged races or other mild physical contact games may not be a good idea.

☛ Like third and fourth graders, they're aware of the opposite sex. But that awareness is no longer mild contempt. There may be some teasing, showing off, etc. It's the beginning of flirtation.

Combining classes works well at this level. That is, if your school has three sixth-grade classes, consider combining them in the gym for one big party. Putting several classes together doesn't seem to work well before grades five and six. In kindergarten through second grade, you want to keep the parties small just to enjoy the kids. And parties for third and fourth graders get so intense, you probably don't want a large group. Fifth and sixth graders can handle it, however, and it can be a great break from the routine.

Fifth and sixth graders are passionate about their music, so you might want to consider tapes and CDs as background music for the party—playing their music, not yours, of course. This is non-traditional classroom stuff, so they'll love it.

Snacks Advice

It's time for MEGASNACKS! These kids get hungry. I wouldn't devote any money to fancy plates, cups and napkins. Spend it all on the food.

☛ Fifth and sixth graders seem to prefer salty snacks to sweet ones.

☛ At last, you can serve the snacks buffet-style. These students are pourers who still, occasionally, spill. But now they can get their own drinks.

My favorites

☛ Halloween: Build your own nachos. All you really need are tortilla chips, a crock pot of melted cheese, and maybe a few toppings: jalapeno peppers, refried beans, green onions, etc.

☛ Winter party: Gingerbread houses—Get the kids to save their small rectangular milk cartons from lunch. (Maybe save them for a few days to be sure there are enough; and, of course, be sure that they're washed.) Each milk carton is the frame of a house. The walls are graham crackers that you stick to the carton with frosting. And those can be decorated with more frosting, candy, sprinkles, chocolate squares, whatever. We recently did this in a fifth grade party, and they loved it. And, yes, they picked the snack themselves in a party committee. It was so fun and so detailed, though, that it doubled as a snack and a craft.

☛ Valentine's Day: How about the infamous smorgasbord sundaes? For a full explanation of those, please see pages 27-28. But in a nutshell, poll the class for favorite toppings for vanilla ice cream. Get the kids to bring the toppings they volunteer, and let them build their own ice-cream sundaes.

CRAFTS ADVICE

Crafts are low-priority in grades five and six. Few activities that can be done in only 10 minutes are sophisticated enough for this age group. The kids would rather socialize.

MY FAVORITES

☛ I get a little non-traditional in crafts for this age group. For a craft, especially at Valentine's Day, perhaps let the kids bring their own music and allow them to dedicate specific songs to whomever they please.

☛ For an end of the year party for sixth graders, I once worked with a group of room parents to create "memory books." We prepared a questionnaire that each child completed, and then the room parents wrote a paragraph about each child. We compiled them in a small book, which, with today's desktop publishing programs, wasn't hard. We distributed them at the party and, I'm willing to bet, gave the kids some keepsakes that they'll cherish for a long time.

GAMES ADVICE

No paper-work games or any that involve heavy-duty thinking! Fifth and sixth graders have been writing and thinking all day. That's lost its novelty, and they're ready to let their hair down.

MY FAVORITES

☛ Halloween seat game: The Spider Web—See pages 24-25. Basically, while the kids are at the parade, you string yarn all through the room. Each child grabs one end of a strand and traces it to its source. Obviously, this is more of a semi-quiet game than a true seat game.

☛ Halloween relay: Toilet Paper Over and Under - As described on page 29. Don't ask me to explain the huge popularity of this one. With more toilet paper, you can also divide the class into groups of three or four and have each group wrap a group member with the toilet paper; it's a mummy-wrap competition.

☞ Winter party seat game: Winter Tray—Display several winter-related items on a tray or small table. Let all the kids see them, and then cover them. Have them write down as many as they can recall. This can be a good game for small teams, especially since teams can ease the thinking burden for these weary minds.

☞ Winter relay: Rubber Gloves and Candy: The object is to unwrap a piece of candy while wearing rubber gloves. (It's harder than it sounds.) Once that's done, the unwrapper can eat the candy but must return to tag a teammate, who then puts on the gloves and attacks the candy. First team to have all members unwrap a candy piece wins.

☞ Valentine's Day seat game: Continuing the song dedications from the crafts section works best for me.

☞ Valentine's Day relay: You may not believe this, but charades never miss. Get one team to think up and enact a song or movie title, and let the other team guess away.

CHAPTER NINE

Common Questions and Answers

WHEN DOES THE PARTY START?

The classroom party usually occurs during the last hour of the school day.

HOW LONG DO ROOM PARTIES LAST?

Room parties usually last one hour.

HOW EARLY SHOULD I GET THERE?

Fifteen minutes before the party at the very earliest. You don't want to be a distraction during class time.

WHAT ARE THE STANDARD ROOM PARTIES?

Halloween, Winter and Valentine's Day.

ARE PARTIES EXPENSIVE?

Not if you spread the word and spread the work. Recruit a lot of suppliers, and no one will feel the pinch.

WHAT IF A GAME OR CRAFT JUST ISN'T WORKING?

Gracefully break away from it and move on to Plan B. But don't forget how flexible the kids are. Ask them for an on-the-spot improvement, and if their suggestion works, go with it.

WHAT IF THE ACTIVITIES FINISH BEFORE THE HOUR DOES?

Try to have five relay games ready, though I bet you'll use only two. Most of those extra games can be variations on the basic relays you've chosen.

CAN I BE A ROOM PARENT EVEN IF I CAN'T ATTEND THE PARTIES?

Absolutely! Parents who supply the snacks or the crafts materials are essential. Without you, there's no party.

WILL I HAVE ANY HELP?

Yes. Remember to spread the word and spread the work. With just a little preparation, you'll have plenty of help.

WILL THE TEACHER BE THERE?

Yes, but give that hard-working professional a break. Please don't expect him or her to help during the party. Fortunately, the teacher will be there to handle any discipline problems.

HOW MANY ROOM PARENTS ARE NEEDED IN THE CLASSROOM?

Three will be fine.

WHAT SHOULD I WEAR?

Wear whatever you're most comfortable in, maybe even a Halloween costume for Halloween. Dress is usually informal.

DOES THE PARTY HAVE TO BE IN THE CLASSROOM?

No, but get permission from the teacher and other appropriate people if you want to go somewhere else. How about the school gym?

WHAT'S THE BEST ADVICE FOR A SUCCESSFUL ROOM PARTY?

Be flexible and adaptable. Listen to what the kids want. Tell yourself that you're going to have fun because I know that you will. And maybe most important of all, remember why you're doing it. There's someone in that room you love with all your heart. Years later, he or she will remember that you were there. Money can't buy that kind of happy memory.

CONCLUSION

I WON'T SAY GOODBYE, because I hope this truly is the beginning of our work together as room parents. But I will repeat just a few of the key ingredients for a successful room party:

- ☛ Relax! You're going to have fun.
- ☛ Spread the word and spread the work.
- ☛ Be flexible. Have options, and go with the flow of the party.

I hope you'll be so flexible that you'll treat this book as the beginning, not the end, of your ideas for room parties. For example, I've discussed only the three traditional room parties: Halloween, Winter and Valentine's Day. Perhaps other occasions or holidays would be equally appropriate for your school. Maybe St. Patrick's Day, or graduation. Or how about a room party for National Teacher Day? It's the Tuesday of the first full week in May.

Good luck in your room parties and in everything you do for your children! All my best hopes go with you.

PARENTS

Name

Phone